MY BODY

My Eyes

By Lloyd G. Douglas

Welcome Books™

Children's Press®
A Division of Scholastic Inc.
New York / Toronto / London / Auckland / Sydney
Mexico City / New Delhi / Hong Kong
Danbury, Connecticut

Photo Credits: Cover © Ariel Skelley/Corbis; p. 5 © Corbis; p. 7 © Ralph A. Clevenger/Corbis; p. 9 © Warren Morgan/Corbis; p. 11 © Richard T. Nowitz/Corbis; p. 13 © Ann-Marie Weber/Corbis; p. 15 © LWA-Dann Tardif/Corbis; p. 17 © Pixland/SuperStock; p. 19 © Van Parys/Corbis Sygma; p. 21 © Mug Shots/Corbis
Contributing Editor: Shira Laskin
Book Design: Michael de Guzman

Library of Congress Cataloging-in-Publication Data

Douglas, Lloyd G.
     My eyes / by Lloyd G. Douglas.
     p. cm.—(My body)
     Includes index.
     Summary: Simple text introduces the functions of the human eye, as well
     as tools that can help people who have vision problems.
     ISBN 0-516-24060-9 (lib. bdg.)—ISBN 0-516-22127-2 (pbk.)
     1. Eye—Juvenile literature. 2. Vision—Juvenile literature. [1. Eye.
     2. Vision. 3. Senses and sensation.] I. Title. II. Series.

     QP475.7.D68 2003
     612.8'4—dc22
                                                              2003012115

Contents

I have two eyes.

I use my eyes to see.

There are black circles
in my eyes.

They are called **pupils**.

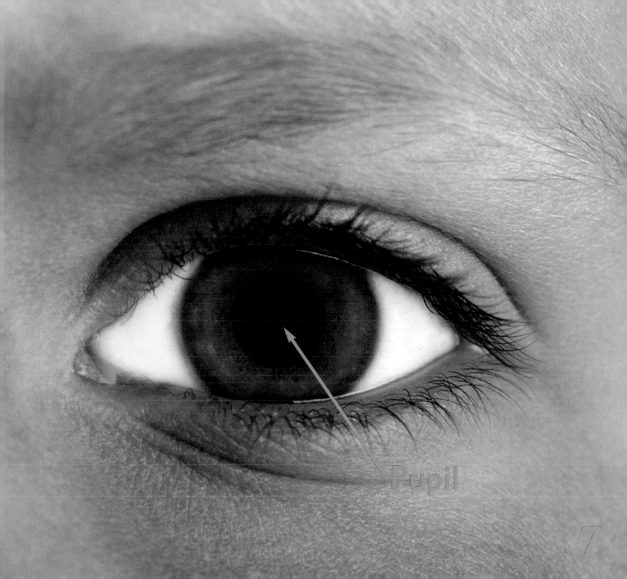

Pupil

7

My pupils let light into my eyes.

This helps me see.

There are **eyelashes** on my **eyelids**.

The eyelashes keep my eyes safe from dirt.

Eyelid

Eyelashes

11

People have different color eyes.

The colored part of my eye is called the **iris**.

Some people cannot
see well.

They wear **glasses** to help
them see.

14

People wear **sunglasses** on sunny days.

Sunglasses keep their eyes safe from the Sun.

Some people cannot see at all.

Guide dogs can help them get from place to place.

19

Our eyes help us to see the world around us.

Eyes are very important parts of our bodies.

New Words

eyelashes (**eye**-lash-iz) short, curved hairs on eyelids that keep eyes safe from dirt

eyelids (**eye**-lihdz) the upper or lower folds of skin that cover the eyes when they are closed

glasses (**glas**-iz) pieces of glass set in frames that people wear to help them see better

guide dogs (**gide dawgz**) dogs trained to lead a person who cannot see

iris (**eye**-riss) the round, colored part of the eye around the pupil

pupils (**pyoo**-puhlz) the round, black part of the eyes that let light come in

sunglasses (suhn-**glas**-iz) dark glasses worn to keep eyes safe from the Sun

To Find Out More

Books
Eyes
by Aleksander Jedrosz
Troll Communications L.L.C.

Sight
by Patricia J. Murphy
Scholastic Library Publishing

Web Site
A Big Look at the Eye
http://kidshealth.org/kid/body
Learn about the eye and its many parts on this Web site.

Index

About the Author
Lloyd G. Douglas has written many books for children.

Reading Consultants
Kris Flynn, Coordinator, Small School District Literacy, The San Diego County Office of Education

Shelly Forys, Certified Reading Recovery Specialist, W.J. Zahnow Elementary School, Waterloo, IL

Paulette Mansell, Certified Reading Recovery Specialist, and Early Literacy Consultant, TX

24